CALIFORNIA

PEARSON LANGUAGE CENTRAL

ELD

Consulting Authors

Jim Cummins, Ph.D.

Lily Wong Fillmore, Ph.D.

Georgia Garcia, Ph.D.

Jill Kerper Mora, Ed.D.

PEARSON

Glenview, Illinois • Boston, Massachusetts • Chandler, Arizona •
Upper Saddle River, New Jersey

ISBN13: 978-0-328-37801-2
ISBN10: 0-328-37801-1

7 8 9 10 V 011 12
CC1

Animal and Plant Characteristics—Look at Us!

Flowers

Vocabulary

flowers

plants

grow

inside

How are flowers unique?

ELA R1.18 Describe common objects and events in both general and specific language. (ELD R.B3)

47

Picture Dictionary

carnation

daisy

lily

rose

sunflower

tulip

· ·

Draw Draw a flower.

ELA R1.17 Identify and sort common words in basic categories (e.g., colors, shapes, foods). (ELD R.B4)

✏ **Circle** Circle *have*.

Flowers have petals.

✏ **Circle** Circle *is*.

The rose is red.

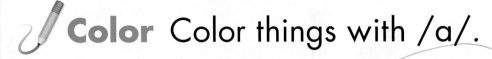 **Color** Color things with /a/.

ELA R1.14 Match all consonant and short-vowel sounds to appropriate letters. (ELD R.B10)

Draw

ELA LS. 1.2 Share information and ideas, speaking audibly in complete, coherent sentences. (ELD LS.B1)

51

home

honeybees

neighbors

orange

Why do animals dig?

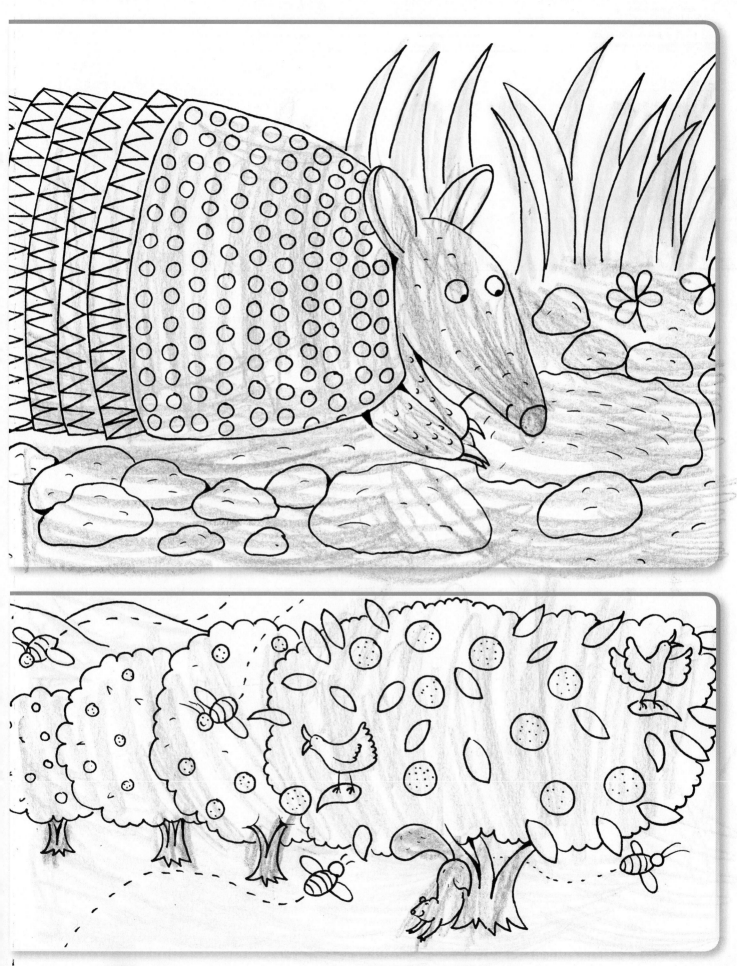

ELA R1.18 Describe common objects and events in both general and specific language. (ELD R.B3)

53

Picture Dictionary

apple

banana

grapes

orange

pear

watermelon

✏️ **Draw** Draw fruit.

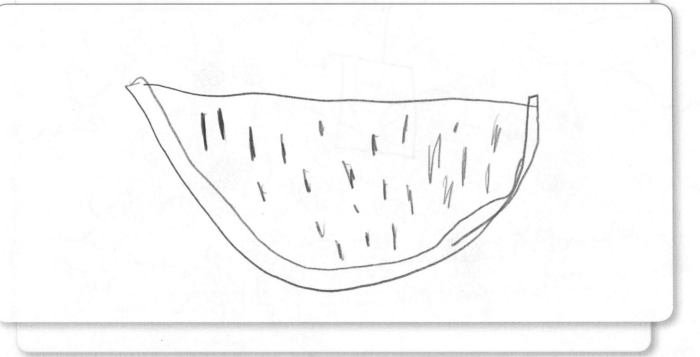

🐻 **ELA R1.17** Identify and sort common words in basic categories (e.g., colors, shapes, foods). (ELD R.B4)

Circle Circle *have.*

Armadillos have claws to dig.

Circle Circle *is.*

An armadillo is digging.

 **Color** Color pictures with /s/.

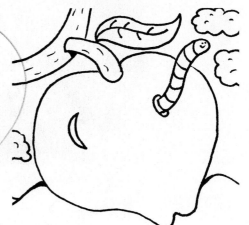

ELA R1.11 Distinguish orally stated one-syllable words and separate into beginning or ending sounds. (ELD R.B10)

✏️ **Draw**

ELA LS. 1.2 Share information and ideas, speaking audibly in complete, coherent sentences. (ELD LS.B1)

57

giraffe

kangaroo

lion

zebra

What kind of animals live in the grasslands?

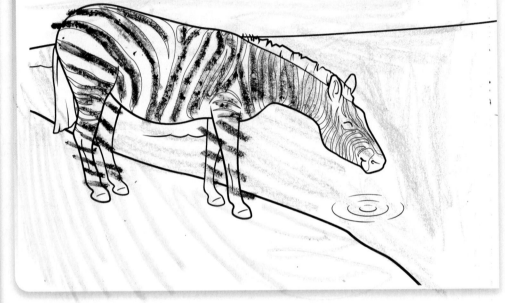

 ELA LS 2.1 Describe people, places, things (e.g., size, color, shape), locations, and actions. (ELD R.B2)

59

Picture Dictionary

chick

colt

kitten

lamb

piglet

puppy

✏️ **Match** Match babies with adults.

ELA R1.17 Identify and sort common words in basic categories (e.g., colors, shapes, foods). (ELD R.B4)

Circle Circle *We.*
We saw the pups play.

Circle Circle *my.*
Prairie dogs are my favorite animal.

Circle Circle *like.*
I like prairie dogs.

Color Color pictures with /p/.

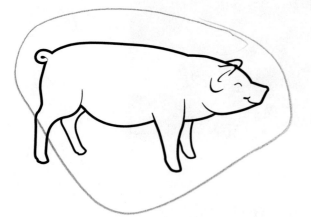

ELA R1.14 Match all consonant and short-vowel sounds to appropriate letters. (ELD R.B10)

✏️ **Draw**

ELA LS. 1.2 Share information and ideas, speaking audibly in complete, coherent sentences. (ELD LS.B1)

63

bear

snores

Where does a bear hibernate?

 ELA LS. 2.1 Describe people, places, things (e.g., size, color, shape), locations, and actions. (ELD LS.B3)

65

Picture Dictionary

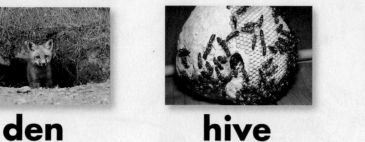

den

hive

hole

log

nest

tree

✏️ **Draw** Draw an animal home.

  ELA R1.17 Identify and sort common words in basic categories (e.g., colors, shapes, foods). (ELD R.B4)

 Circle Circle *We.*

We saw a bear in a cave.

 Circle Circle *my.*

Bears are my favorite animal.

✏️ **Circle** Circle things with /k/.

ELA R1.14 Match all consonant and short-vowel sounds to appropriate letters. (ELD R.B10)

 **Draw**

 ELA LS. 1.2 Share information and ideas, speaking audibly in complete, coherent sentences. (ELD LS.B1)

69

bed

burrow

cave

winter

What kind of home does an animal need?

ELA LS 2.1 Describe people, places, things (e.g., size, color, shape), locations, and actions. (ELD LS.B3)

71

Picture Dictionary

top ▶

over ⬇

bottom ▶

under ⬆

✏ **Circle** Circle the top of the cave.

✏ **Circle** Circle the frog over the log.

ELA R1.17 Identify and sort common words in basic categories (e.g., colors, shapes, foods). (ELD R.B4)

Circle Circle *He.*

He saw a dormouse sleeping.

Circle Circle *for.*

Chipmunks build homes for winter.

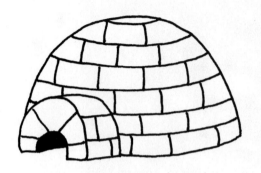 **Circle** Circle things with /i/.

ELA R1.14 Match all consonant and short-vowel sounds to appropriate letters. (ELD R.B1)

 **Draw**

 ELA LS. 1.2 Share information and ideas, speaking audibly in complete, coherent sentences. (ELD LS.B1)

75

Vocabulary

swim

swing

How do animals move?

ELA LS 2.1 Describe people, places, things (e.g., size, color, shape), locations, and actions. (ELD LS.B3)

77

Picture Dictionary

climb

hop

jump

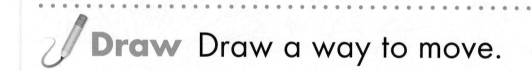

run

skip

walk

✏️ **Draw** Draw a way to move.

 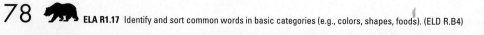 **ELA R1.17** Identify and sort common words in basic categories (e.g., colors, shapes, foods). (ELD R.B4)

✎ **Circle** Circle *He.*

He saw a fox dig a hole.

✎ **Circle** Circle *for.*

Meerkats dig for food.

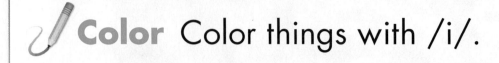

Color Color things with /i/.

ELA R1.14 Match all consonant and short-vowel sounds to appropriate letters. (ELD R.B1)

How do animals move?

Draw

 ELA LS. 1.2 Share information and ideas, speaking audibly in complete, coherent sentences. (ELD LS.B1)

Changes–Changes All Around Us

THE BIG ?

How do changes affect us?

Moving Away
What happens when a friend moves away?

Getting Older
What new things can you do as you get older?

American Heroes
What can we learn from people in the past?

Friends Change
How do friendships change?

Things Change
How was the past different from today?

Feelings Change
How can we change the way we feel?

Changes—Changes All Around Us

Vocabulary

called

play

shared

word

What happens when a friend moves away?

84

 ELA LS 2.3 Relate an experience or creative story in a logical sequence. (ELD LS.B3)

85

Picture Dictionary

grandpa   **father**

grandma →   ← **mother**

sister   **brother**

. . . .

Draw Draw your family.

✏️ **Circle** Circle *She.* Circle *me.*
She told me goodbye.

✏️ **Circle** Circle *with.*
I can not play with my friend.

✏️ **Circle** Circle pictures with /n/.

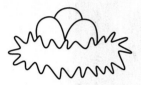  

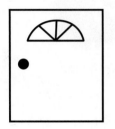  

✏️ **Circle** Circle pictures with /b/.

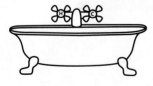  

🐻 **ELA R1.14** Match all consonant and short-vowel sounds to appropriate letters. (ELD R.B10)

 Draw

 ELA LS. 1.2 Share information and ideas, speaking audibly in complete, coherent sentences. (ELD LS.B1)

89

Vocabulary

duck

water

What new things can you do as you get older?

ELA LS 2.3 Relate an experience or creative story in a logical sequence. (ELD LS.B3)

91

Picture Dictionary

happy

sad

scared

excited

- -

✏ **Draw** Draw feelings.

happy

sad

🐻 **ELA R1.17** Identify and sort common words in basic categories (e.g., colors, shapes, foods). (ELD R.B4)

 Circle Circle *with*. Circle *me*.
You ride with me.

 Circle Circle *She*.
She rides without help.

Color Color pictures with /r/.

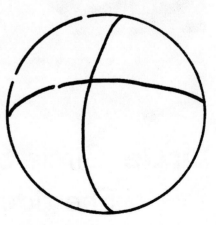

ELA R1.14 Match all consonant and short-vowel sounds to appropriate letters. (ELD R.B1)

What new things can you do as you get older?

 **Draw**

ELA LS. 1.2 Share information and ideas, speaking audibly in complete, coherent sentences. (ELD LS.B1)

crowds

hero

sign

storm

What can we learn from people in the past?

 ELA LS 2.1 Describe people, places, things (e.g., size, color, shape), locations, and actions. (ELD LS.B3)

97

Picture Dictionary

bell

blacksmith

cottage

horse

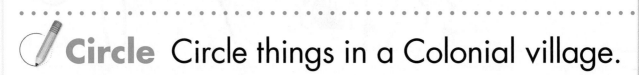

✏️ **Circle** Circle things in a Colonial village.

🐻 **ELA R1.17** Identify and sort common words in basic categories (e.g., colors, shapes, foods). (ELD R.B4)

✐ **Circle** Circle *see.*

I see Lincoln's hat.

✐ **Circle** Circle *Look.*

Look at Ben Franklin work.

Circle Circle pictures with /d/.

Circle Circle pictures with /k/.

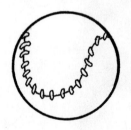

 ELA R1.14 Match all consonant and short-vowel sounds to appropriate letters. (ELD R.B10)

 Draw

 ELA LS. 1.2 Share information and ideas, speaking audibly in complete, coherent sentences. (ELD LS.B1)

101

Vocabulary

friends

game

How do friendships change?

 ELA LS 2.3 Relate an experience or creative story in a logical sequence. (ELD LS.B3)

103

Animal Body Coverings

Picture Dictionary

feathers   **fur**   **quills**

scales   **shell**

 **Circle** Circle an animal with feathers.

Circle Circle an animal with a shell.

104 ELA R1.17 Identify and sort common words in basic categories (e.g., colors, shapes, foods). (ELD R.B4)

✏️ **Circle** Circle *see*.

I see my friend after school.

✏️ **Circle** Circle *Look*.

Look at the friends playing.

 ELA R1.15 Read simple one-syllable and high-frequency words (i.e., sight words). (ELD R.B2)

 **Color** Color pictures with /f/.

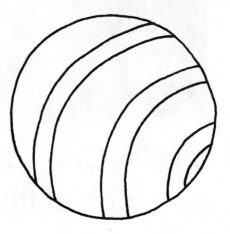

How do friendships change?

✏️ **Draw**

 ELA LS. 1.2 Share information and ideas, speaking audibly in complete, coherent sentences.

107

Things Change

Vocabulary

camera

news

How was the past different from today?

ELA R 1.18 Describe common objects and events in both general and specific language. (ELD R.B4)

109

Picture Dictionary

book   **calendar**   **crayons**

desk   **paper**   **pencil**

Draw Draw things in a classroom.

 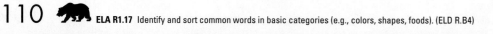 **ELA R1.17** Identify and sort common words in basic categories (e.g., colors, shapes, foods). (ELD R.B4)

🖊 **Circle** Circle *They*.

They were in one classroom.

🖊 **Circle** Circle *you*.

Today you can use a computer.

🖊 **Circle** Circle *of*.

All of us go to school now.

Color Color things with /o/.

ELA R1.14 Match all consonant and short-vowel sounds to appropriate letters. (ELD R.B10)

 Draw

 ELA LS. 1.2 Share information and ideas, speaking audibly in complete, coherent sentences.

113

roar

strong

How can we change the way we feel?

 ELA LS 2.3 Relate an experience or creative story in a logical sequence. (ELD LS.B3)

115

Picture Dictionary

mouth

tail

legs

paws

✏️ **Circle** Circle the tail.

✏️ **Circle** Circle a paw.

ELA R1.17 Identify and sort common words in basic categories (e.g., colors, shapes, foods). (ELD R.B4)

 Circle Circle *They.*
They were good friends.

 Circle Circle *you.* Circle *of.*
Friends take care of you.

Circle Circle things with /o/.

ELA R1.14 Match all consonant and short-vowel sounds to appropriate letters. (ELD R.B10)

 Draw

 ELA LS. 1.2 Share information and ideas, speaking audibly in complete, coherent sentences.

119

Adventures— Let's Go Exploring

THE BIG

Where will our adventures take us?

Unit 4

A Day's Adventures
What adventures can you have every day?

A Lucky Day
What adventures can you have on a lucky day?

Animal Adventures
What adventures can animals have?

Goldilocks's Adventures
What kind of adventures can a child have?

Cold Adventures
What is it like in the Antarctic?

City Adventures
What are some city adventures?

bunnies

clock

nap

play

rabbit

What adventures can you have every day?

 ELA LS 2.3 Relate an experience or creative story in a logical sequence. (ELD LS.B3)

123

Picture Dictionary

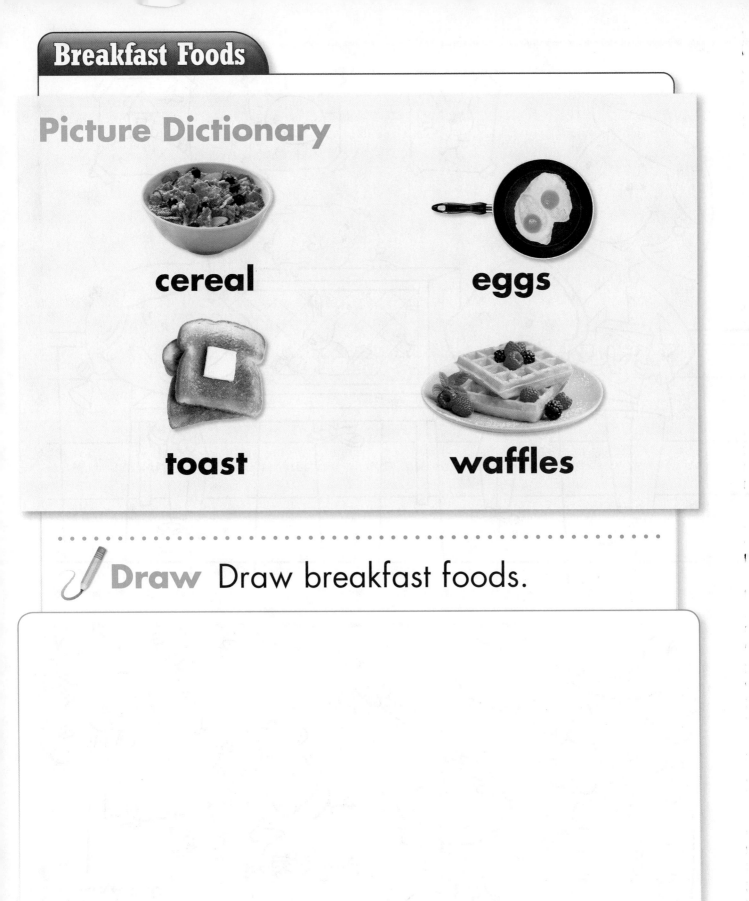

cereal

eggs

toast

waffles

✏️ **Draw** Draw breakfast foods.

ELA R1.17 Identify and sort common words in basic categories (e.g., colors, shapes, foods). (ELD R.B4)

 Circle Circle *are.*

We are happy to have a class pet.

Circle Circle *do.* Circle *that.*

We do projects that are fun.

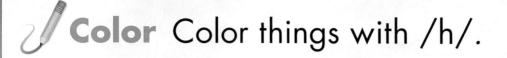 **Color** Color things with /h/.

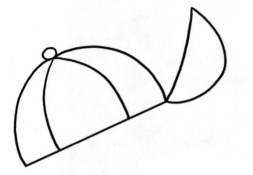

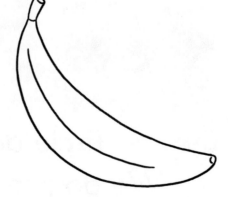

ELA R1.14 Match all consonant and short-vowel sounds to appropriate letters. (ELD R.B10)

 **Draw**

 ELA LS. 1.2 Share information and ideas, speaking audibly in complete, coherent sentences. (ELD LS.B3)

127

A Lucky Day

Vocabulary

bath

dinner

rabbit

What adventures can you have on a lucky day?

 ELA LS 2.3 Relate an experience or creative story in a logical sequence. (ELD LS.B3)

129

Picture Dictionary

pizza   **salad**   **sandwich**

soup   **spaghetti**   **stew**

🖍 **Draw** Draw dinner foods.

 Circle Circle *are*. Circle *do*.
We do things that are special.

 Circle Circle *That*.
That is lucky!

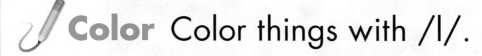 **Color** Color things with /l/.

 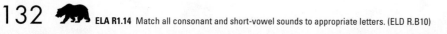 **ELA R1.14** Match all consonant and short-vowel sounds to appropriate letters. (ELD R.B10)

 **Draw**

ELA LS. 1.2 Share information and ideas, speaking audibly in complete, coherent sentences. (ELD LS.B2)

133

Animal Adventures

cottontails

mouse

snakes

squirrels

frogs

What adventures can animals have?

 ELA LS 2.3 Relate an experience or creative story in a logical sequence. (ELD LS.B3)

135

Picture Dictionary

small

large

short

tall

✏️ **Circle** Circle a thing that is small.

✏️ **Circle** Circle a thing that is tall.

 ELA R1.17 Identify and sort common words in basic categories (e.g., colors, shapes, foods). (ELD R.B4)

✏️ **Circle** Circle *One*. Circle *two*.
One squirrel will eat two acorns.

✏️ **Circle** Circle *Three*.
Three birds live in the tree.

✏️ **Circle** Circle *Four*. Circle *five*.
Four or five birds can live in the tree.

Circle Circle the beginning sounds.

/tr/   /cr/

/sp/   /sk/

Circle Circle the ending sounds.

/nd/   /ft/

/st/   /sk/

ELA R1.14 Match all consonant and short-vowel sounds to appropriate letters. (ELD R.B10)

Draw

 ELA LS. 1.2 Share information and ideas, speaking audibly in complete, coherent sentences. (ELD LS.B1)

139

Vocabulary

baby

father

mother

woods

What kind of adventures can a child have?

 ELA R 2.4 Retell familiar stories. (ELD R.B7)

141

Furniture

Picture Dictionary

bed

chair

table

dresser

✏️ **Draw** Draw furniture.

ELA R1.17 Identify and sort common words in basic categories (e.g., colors, shapes, foods). (ELD R.B4)

 Circle Circle *One*. Circle *three*.
One girl visited three bears.

 Circle Circle *two*.
She saw two squirrels in the woods.

 Circle Circle *four*. Circle *five*.
She saw four or five birds.

 **Circle** Circle things with /g/.

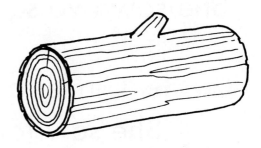

ELA R1.14 Match all consonant and short-vowel sounds to appropriate letters. (ELD R.B10)

 **Draw**

 ELA LS. 1.2 Share information and ideas, speaking audibly in complete, coherent sentences. (ELD LS.B1)

145

penguin

ship

sled

thunder

What is it like in the Antarctic?

ELA LS 1.2 Share information and ideas, speaking audibly in complete, coherent sentences. (ELD LS.B2)

147

Picture Dictionary

hot

cold

warm

freezing

 Match Match temperatures.

cold

hot

ELA R1.17 Identify and sort common words in basic categories (e.g., colors, shapes, foods). (ELD R.B4)

 Circle Circle *from*. Circle *here*.
Start sledding from here.

 Circle Circle *go*.
Penguins go sledding too.

✏️ **Color** Color things with /e/.

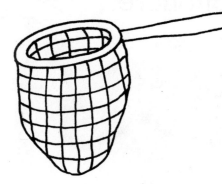

  ELA R1.14 Match all consonant and short-vowel sounds to appropriate letters. (ELD R.B10)

What is it like in the Antarctic?

 **Draw**

 ELA LS. 1.2 Share information and ideas, speaking audibly in complete, coherent sentences. (ELD LS.B1)

151

Vocabulary

bread

grandma

park

What are some city adventures?

 ELA LS 1.2 Share information and ideas, speaking audibly in complete, coherent sentences. (ELD LS.B2)

153

Picture Dictionary

clouds

moon

stars

sun

Draw Draw things in the sky.

ELA R1.17 Identify and sort common words in basic categories (e.g., colors, shapes, foods). (ELD R.B4)

 Circle Circle *Here.*

Here is the city market.

 Circle Circle *Go.* Circle *from.*

Go from the museum to the park.

Circle Circle things with /e/.

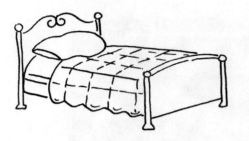

ELA R1.14 Match all consonant and short-vowel sounds to appropriate letters. (ELD R.B10)

What are some city adventures?

 Draw

 ELA LS. 1.2 Share information and ideas, speaking audibly in complete, coherent sentences. (ELD LS.B1)

157

Transportation— Going Places

THE BIG ?

How do people get from here to there?

Unit 5

Getting Places
What are some forms of transportation?

Help in an Emergency
What kinds of transportation help us in an emergency?

Going Places at Work
How does transportation help at work?

Trains
How does a train get over a mountain?

Ways to Travel
How do people around the world travel?

Ways to Get to School
How do children get to school?

bus

train

What are some forms of transportation?

ELA R 1.18 Describe common objects and events in both general and specific language. (ELD R.B2)

161

Picture Dictionary

boat

car

train

truck

✏️ **Draw** Draw a kind of transportation.

ELA R1.17 Identify and sort common words in basic categories (e.g., colors, shapes, foods). (ELD R.B4)

 Circle Circle *yellow*.
The plane was near a yellow line.

 Circle Circle *green*. Circle *blue*.
A green plane flew in the blue sky.

✏️ **Circle** Circle things with /j/.

✏️ **Circle** Circle things with /w/.

🐻 **ELA R1.14** Match all consonant and short-vowel sounds to appropriate letters. (ELD R.B1)

✎ Draw

 ELA LS. 1.2 Share information and ideas, speaking audibly in complete, coherent sentences. (ELD LS.B3)

165

Vocabulary

boat

swimmer

taxi

What kinds of transportation help us in an emergency?

ELA R 1.18 Describe common objects and events in both general and specific language. (ELD R.B2)

167

Picture Dictionary

Coast Guard

firefighters

nurse

police

✏️ **Draw** Draw someone who helps us.

 ELA R1.17 Identify and sort common words in basic categories (e.g., colors, shapes, foods). (ELD R.B4)

 Circle Circle *yellow*. Circle *blue*.
A yellow boat was in the blue water.

 Circle Circle *green*.
They saved a green turtle.

Circle Circle things with /ks/.

ELA R1.14 Match all consonant and short-vowel sounds to appropriate letters. (ELD R.B10)

 **Draw**

 ELA LS. 1.2 Share information and ideas, speaking audibly in complete, coherent sentences. (ELD LS.B3)

171

parking lots

rain

tunnels

bike

snow

sun

wind

How does transportation help at work?

 ELA R 1.18 Describe common objects and events in both general and specific language. (ELD R.B2)

173

Picture Dictionary

astronaut

bike messenger

cashier

mechanic

teacher

writer

Draw Draw someone doing a job.

  ELA R1.17 Identify and sort common words in basic categories (e.g., colors, shapes, foods). (ELD R.B4)

✏️ **Circle** Circle *what*.

The messenger knows what to wear.

✏️ **Circle** Circle *said*. Circle *was*.

He said the mask was warm.

Color Color things with /u/.

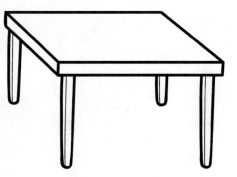

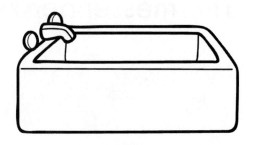

ELA R1.14 Match all consonant and short-vowel sounds to appropriate letters. (ELD R.B1)

✎ **Draw**

ELA LS. 1.2 Share information and ideas, speaking audibly in complete, coherent sentences. (ELD LS.B3)

177

Trains

Vocabulary

dining cars

dolls

sleeping cars

load
switching
toys
wheels

How does a train get over a mountain?

ELA R 1.18 Describe common objects and events in both general and specific language. (ELD R.B2)

179

Picture Dictionary

ball

blocks

doll

puzzle

stuffed animal

top

· ·

 Draw Draw toys.

ELA R1.17 Identify and sort common words in basic categories (e.g., colors, shapes, foods). (ELD R.B4)

 Circle Circle *said*. Circle *what*.
The little engine said what it could do.

 Circle Circle *was*.
The little engine was trying hard.

Circle Circle things with /u/.

ELA R1.14 Match all consonant and short-vowel sounds to appropriate letters. (ELD R.B1)

 **Draw**

 ELA LS. 1.2 Share information and ideas, speaking audibly in complete, coherent sentences. (ELD LS.B1)

183

Vocabulary

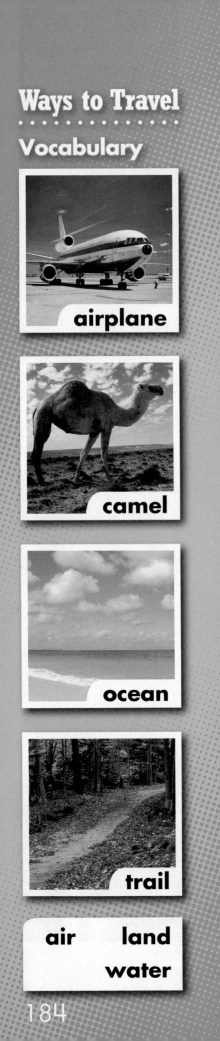

airplane

camel

ocean

trail

air   land
water

How do people around the world travel?

ELA R 1.18 Describe common objects and events in both general and specific language. (ELD R.B3)

185

Picture Dictionary

desert

lake

mountain

river

volcano

waterfall

✏️ **Draw** Draw a place in the world.

 Circle Circle *where*.

The driver knew where to go.

 Circle Circle *Come*.

Come see the town.

✏ **Circle** Circle things with /v/.

✏ **Circle** Circle things with /z/.

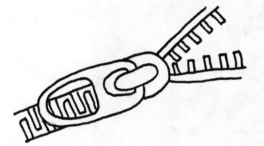

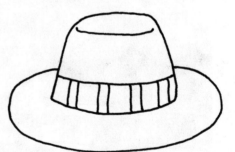

Draw

 ELA LS. 1.2 Share information and ideas, speaking audibly in complete, coherent sentences. (ELD LS.B3)

189

Vocabulary

bicycles

radio

train

bus

car

school

How do children get to school?

 ELA R 1.18 Describe common objects and events in both general and specific language. (ELD R.B4)

191

Picture Dictionary

countryside

farm

town

village

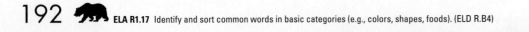

✏️ **Draw** Draw a place to live.

🐻 **ELA R1.17** Identify and sort common words in basic categories (e.g., colors, shapes, foods). (ELD R.B4)

 Circle Circle *where*.

The yak goes where she goes.

 Circle Circle *come*.

We come to school.

✏ Circle Circle things with /y/.

✏ Circle Circle things with /kw/.

 Draw

 ELA LS. 1.2 Share information and ideas, speaking audibly in complete, coherent sentences. (ELD LS.B3)

195

Building—Putting It Together

What are different ways of building?

Building—Putting It Together

Vocabulary

pipes

spills

wires

What do you need to build a school?

ELA R 1.18 Describe common objects and events in both general and specific language. (ELD R.B4)

199

Picture Dictionary

bricks

cement

steel

wood

✏️ **Match** Match building materials.

 ELA R1.17 Identify and sort common words in basic categories (e.g., colors, shapes, foods). (ELD R.B4)

 Circle Circle *He*. Circle *a*. Circle *to*.
He uses a bulldozer to move dirt.

 Circle Circle *Look*. Circle *the*. Circle *go*.
Look at the truck go!

Identify Sounds Aa and Ii

✏️ **Circle** Circle things with /a/.

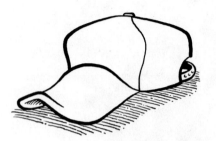

✏️ **Circle** Circle things with /i/.

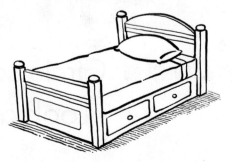

ELA R1.14 Match all consonant and short-vowel sounds to appropriate letters. (ELD R.B10)

 Draw

 ELA LS. 1.2 Share information and ideas, speaking audibly in complete, coherent sentences. (ELD LS.B3)

203

cat

cow

goat

dog
mouse
rooster
sheep

What tools do you need to build things?

ELA R 1.18 Describe common objects and events in both general and specific language. (ELD R.B4)

205

Picture Dictionary

cow

goat

rooster

sheep

· ·

Draw Draw a farm animal.

What can you build with a hammer?

✏️ **Circle** Circle *We.* Circle *are.*
We are making a house.

✏️ **Circle** Circle *Here.* Circle *is.*
Here is the hammer.

 ELA R1.15 Read simple one-syllable and high-frequency words (i.e., sight words). (ELD R.B2)

207

Circle Circle things with /o/.

ELA R1.14 Match all consonant and short-vowel sounds to appropriate letters. (ELD R.B10)

 # What tools do you need to build things?

Draw

 ELA LS. 1.2 Share information and ideas, speaking audibly in complete, coherent sentences. (ELD LS.B3)

209

Vocabulary

kits

mud

pond

teeth

trees

How do beavers build?

ELA R 1.18 Describe common objects and events in both general and specific language. (ELD R.B4)

211

Picture Dictionary

grass

leaves

mud

sticks

✏️ **Circle** Circle what animals use.

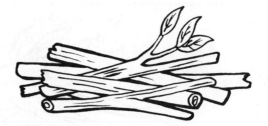

ELA R1.17 Identify and sort common words in basic categories (e.g., colors, shapes, foods). (ELD R.B4)

 Circle Circle *Two*.

Two beavers are swimming.

 Circle Circle *They*. Circle *have*.

They have homes on the water.

Circle Circle things with /e/.

ELA R1.14 Match all consonant and short-vowel sounds to appropriate letters. (ELD R.B10)

 **Draw**

 ELA LS. 1.2 Share information and ideas, speaking audibly in complete, coherent sentences. (ELD LS.B3)

215

Night Workers

Vocabulary

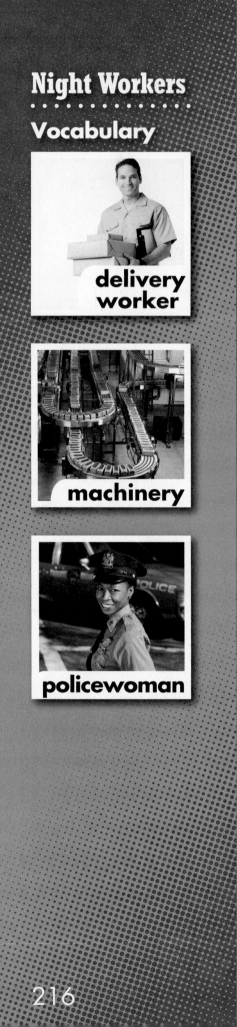

delivery worker

machinery

policewoman

Who works at night?

 ELA R 1.18 Describe common objects and events in both general and specific language. (ELD R.B4)

217

Picture Dictionary

bulldozer   **cement mixer**   **concrete**

crane   **goggles**   **hard hats**

✏️ **Draw** Draw something at a site.

ELA R1.17 Identify and sort common words in basic categories (e.g., colors, shapes, foods). (ELD R.B4)

 Circle Circle *do*. Circle *that*.
A crane can do that.

 Circle Circle *I*. Circle *like*. Circle *see*.
I like to see big trucks.

✏ **Circle** Circle things with /u/.

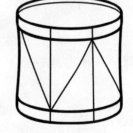

ELA R1.14 Match all consonant and short-vowel sounds to appropriate letters. (ELD R.B10)

 **Draw**

 ELA LS. 1.2 Share information and ideas, speaking audibly in complete, coherent sentences. (ELD LS.B3)

221

construction workers

neighbors

truck driver

Who helps to build a house?

ELA R 1.18 Describe common objects and events in both general and specific language. (ELD R.B4)

223

Picture Dictionary

apartment

house

hut

igloo

teepee

trailer

Draw Draw a home.

ELA R1.17 Identify and sort common words in basic categories (e.g., colors, shapes, foods). (ELD R.B4)

 Circle Circle *Four.*

Four workers built a wall.

 Circle Circle *She.* Circle *was.*

She was laying bricks.

Match Match words with pictures.

bed

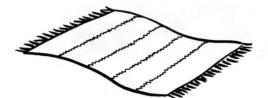

hat

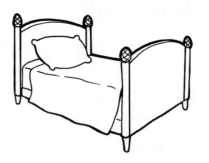

log

rug

pig

ELA R1.15 Read simple one-syllable and high-frequency words (i.e., sight words). (ELD R.B2)

Who helps to build a house?

 **Draw**

 ELA LS. 1.2 Share information and ideas, speaking audibly in complete, coherent sentences. (ELD LS.B3)

227

ant

fall

spring

hundreds
months

How do ants build?

 ELA R 1.18 Describe common objects and events in both general and specific language. (ELD R.B4)

229

Picture Dictionary

bee

beetle

cricket

wasp

✏️ **Draw** Draw an insect.

ELA R1.17 Identify and sort common words in basic categories (e.g., colors, shapes, foods). (ELD R.B4)

✏️ **Circle** Circle *come*.

Worker ants come to dig tunnels.

✏️ **Circle** Circle *One*.

One queen ant lays eggs.

✏️ **Match** Match words with pictures.

   **ant**

   **cup**

   **hen**

   **pig**

   **mop**

ELA R1.15 Read simple one-syllable and high-frequency words (i.e., sight words). (ELD R.B2)

How do ants build?

✏️ **Draw**

 ELA LS. 1.2 Share information and ideas, speaking audibly in complete, coherent sentences. (ELD LS.B3)

233

Picture Glossary

Colors

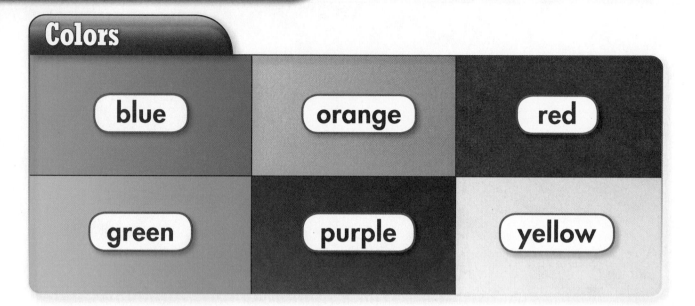

blue

orange

red

green

purple

yellow

Numbers

1	one	
2	two	
3	three	
4	four	
5	five	
6	six	
7	seven	
8	eight	
9	nine	
10	ten	

Clothing

dress	hat	pants
shoes	shorts	t-shirt

Weather

jacket	raincoat	rainy
snowy	sunny	umbrella

Family

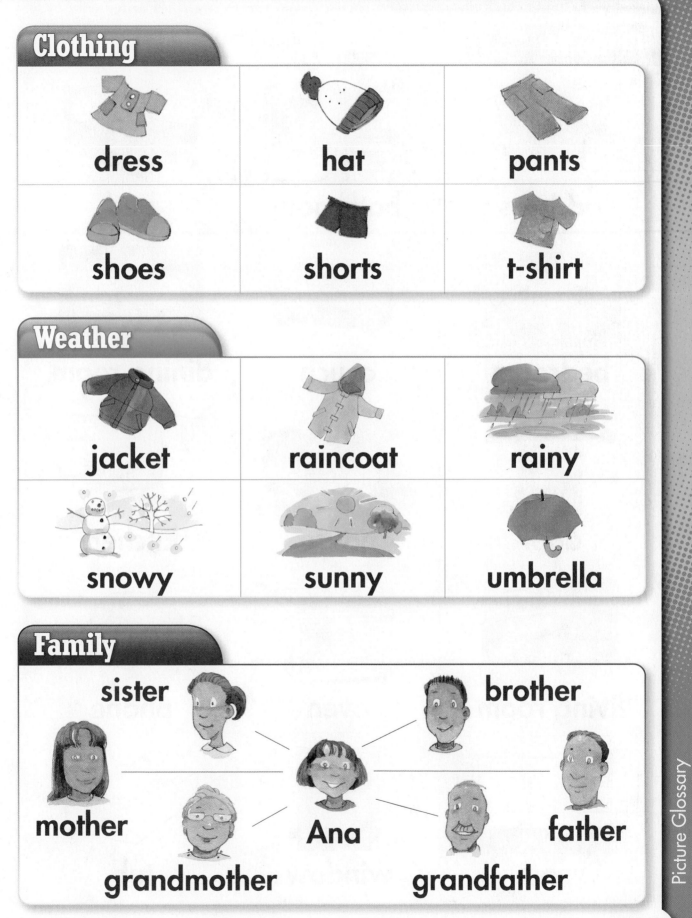

sister   brother

mother   Ana   father

grandmother   grandfather

Picture Glossary

At Home

52 Elm St. **address**	**bathroom**	**bed**
bedroom	**couch**	**dining room**
door	**house**	**kitchen**
living room	**oven**	**phone**
room	**window**	**tub**

236

adding

book

chair

crayon

desk

globe

map

painting

pencil

reading

story

table

working on the computer

writing

ENGLISH-LANGUAGE ARTS

Reading Standards

1.0 Word Analysis, Fluency, and Systematic Vocabulary Development

Students know about letters, words, and sounds. They apply this knowledge to read simple sentences.

Concepts About Print

1.1 Identify the front cover, back cover, and title page of a book.

1.2 Follow words from left to right and from top to bottom on the printed page.

1.3 Understand that printed materials provide information.

1.4 Recognize that sentences in print are made up of separate words.

1.5 Distinguish letters from words.

1.6 Recognize and name all uppercase and lowercase letters of the alphabet.

Phonemic Awareness

1.7 Track (move sequentially from sound to sound) and represent the number, sameness/difference, and order of two and three isolated phonemes (e.g., /f, s, th/, /j, d, j/).

1.8 Track (move sequentially from sound to sound) and represent changes in simple syllables and words with two and three sounds as one sound is added, substituted, omitted, shifted, or repeated (e.g., vowel-consonant, consonant-vowel, or consonant-vowel-consonant).

1.9 Blend vowel-consonant sounds orally to make words or syllables.

1.10 Identify and produce rhyming words in response to an oral prompt.

1.11 Distinguish orally stated one-syllable words and separate into beginning or ending sounds.

1.12 Track auditorily each word in a sentence and each syllable in a word.

1.13 Count the number of sounds in syllables and syllables in words.

Decoding and Word Recognition

1.14 Match all consonant and short-vowel sounds to appropriate letters.

1.15 Read simple one-syllable and high-frequency words (i.e., sight words).

1.16 Understand that as letters of words change, so do the sounds (i.e., the alphabetic principle).

Vocabulary and Concept Development

1.17 Identify and sort common words in basic categories (e.g., colors, shapes, foods).

1.18 Describe common objects and events in both general and specific language.

2.0 Reading Comprehension

Students identify the basic facts and ideas in what they have read, heard, or viewed. They use comprehension strategies (e.g., generating and responding to questions, comparing new information to what is already known). The selections in *Recommended Literature, Kindergarten Through Grade Twelve* (California Department of Education, 2002) illustrate the quality and complexity of the materials to be read by students.

Structural Features of Informational Materials

2.1 Locate the title, table of contents, name of author, and name of illustrator.

Comprehension and Analysis of Grade-Level-Appropriate Text

2.2 Use pictures and context to make predictions about story content.

2.3 Connect to life experiences the information and events in texts.

2.4 Retell familiar stories.

2.5 Ask and answer questions about essential elements of a text.

3.0 Literary Response and Analysis

Students listen and respond to stories based on well-known characters, themes, plots, and settings. The selections in *Recommended Literature, Kindergarten Through Grade Twelve* illustrate the quality and complexity of the materials to be read by students.

Narrative Analysis of Grade-Level-Appropriate Text

3.1 Distinguish fantasy from realistic text.

3.2 Identify types of everyday print materials (e.g., storybooks, poems, newspapers, signs, labels).

3.3 Identify characters, settings, and important events.

Writing Standards

1.0 Writing Strategies

Students write words and brief sentences that are legible.

Organization and Focus

1.1 Use letters and phonetically spelled words to write about experiences, stories, people, objects, or events.

1.2 Write consonant-vowel-consonant words (i.e., demonstrate the alphabetic principle).
1.3 Write by moving from left to right and from top to bottom.

Penmanship
1.4 Write uppercase and lowercase letters of the alphabet independently, attending to the form and proper spacing of the letters.

Written and Oral English Language Conventions Standards

The standards for written and oral English language conventions have been placed between those for writing and for listening and speaking because these conventions are essential to both sets of skills.

1.0 Written and Oral English Language Conventions

Students write and speak with a command of standard English conventions.

Sentence Structure
1.1 Recognize and use complete, coherent sentences when speaking.

Spelling
1.2 Spell independently by using pre-phonetic knowledge, sounds of the alphabet, and knowledge of letter names.

Listening and Speaking Standards

1.0 Listening and Speaking Strategies

Students listen and respond to oral communication. They speak in clear and coherent sentences.

Comprehension
1.1 Understand and follow one- and two-step oral directions.
1.2 Share information and ideas, speaking audibly in complete, coherent sentences.

2.0 Speaking Applications (Genres and Their Characteristics)

Students deliver brief recitations and oral presentations about familiar experiences or interests, demonstrating command of the organization and delivery strategies outlined in Listening and Speaking Standard 1.0.

Using the listening and speaking strategies of kindergarten outlined in Listening and Speaking Standard 1.0, students:
2.1 Describe people, places, things (e.g., size, color, shape), locations, and actions.

2.2 Recite short poems, rhymes, and songs.
2.3 Relate an experience or creative story in a logical sequence.

ENGLISH-LANGUAGE DEVELOPMENT

Reading Standards

Beginning

Word Analysis
B1. Recognize English phonemes that correspond to phonemes students already hear and produce in their primary language.

Fluency and Systematic Vocabulary Development
B2. Read aloud simple words (e.g., nouns and adjectives) in stories or games.
B3. Respond appropriately to some social and academic interactions (e.g., simple question/answer, negotiate play).
B4. Demonstrate comprehension of simple vocabulary with an appropriate action.
B5. Retell simple stories by using drawings, words, or phrases.
B6. Produce simple vocabulary (single words or short phrases) to communicate basic needs in social and academic settings (e.g., locations, greetings, classroom objects).

Reading Comprehension
B7. Respond orally to stories read aloud, using physical actions and other means of nonverbal communication (e.g., matching objects, pointing to an answer, drawing pictures).
B8. Respond orally to stories read aloud, giving one- or two-word responses (e.g., "brown bear") to factual comprehension questions.
B9. Draw pictures from one's own experience related to a story or topic (e.g., community in social studies).
B10. Understand and follow simple one-step directions for classroom activities.
B11. Identify, using key words or pictures, the basic sequence of events in stories read aloud.

Literary Response and Analysis
B12. Listen to a story and respond orally in one or two words to factual comprehension questions.
B13. Draw pictures related to a work of literature identifying setting and characters.

Early Intermediate

Word Analysis

EI1. Produce English phonemes that correspond to phonemes students already hear and produce, including long and short vowels and initial and final consonants.

EI2. Recognize English phonemes that do not correspond to sounds students hear and produce, (e.g., *a* in *cat* and final consonants).

Fluency and Systematic Vocabulary Development

EI3. Produce vocabulary, phrases, and simple sentences to communicate basic needs in social and academic settings.

EI4. Read simple vocabulary, phrases, and sentences independently.

EI5. Read aloud an increasing number of English words.

EI6. Demonstrate internalization of English grammar, usage, and word choice by recognizing and correcting some errors when speaking or reading aloud.

Reading Comprehension

EI7. Respond orally to simple stories read aloud, using phrases or simple sentences to answer factual comprehension questions.

EI8. Draw and label pictures related to a story topic or one's own experience.

EI9. Understand and follow simple two-step directions for classroom activities.

EI10. Orally identify, using key words or phrases, the basic sequence of events in text read aloud.

EI11. Draw logical inferences from a story read aloud.

Literary Response and Analysis

EI12. Respond orally to factual comprehension questions about stories by answering in simple sentences.

EI13. Recite simple poems.

EI14. Identify orally the setting and characters by using simple sentences and vocabulary.

Intermediate

Word Analysis

I1. Pronounce most English phonemes correctly while reading aloud.

I2. Recognize sound/symbol relationships and basic word-formation rules in phrases, simple sentences, or simple text.

I3. Recognize and name all uppercase and lowercase letters of the alphabet.

Fluency and Systematic Vocabulary Development

I4. Demonstrate internalization of English grammar, usage, and word choice by recognizing and correcting errors when speaking or reading aloud.

I5. Use decoding skills to read more complex words independently.

I6. Use more complex vocabulary and sentences to communicate needs and express ideas in a wider variety of social and academic settings (e.g., classroom discussions, mediation of conflicts).

I7. Apply knowledge of content-related vocabulary to discussions and reading.

I8. Recognize simple prefixes and suffixes when they are attached to known vocabulary (e.g., *remove, jumping*).

Reading Comprehension

I9. Read stories and respond orally in simple sentences to factual comprehension questions about the stories.

I10. While reading aloud in a group, point out basic text features, such as the title, table of contents, and chapter headings.

I11. Draw inferences about stories read aloud and use simple phrases or sentences to communicate the inferences.

I12. Write captions or phrases for drawings related to a story.

I13. Understand and follow some multiple-step directions for classroom-related activities.

Literary Response and Analysis

I14. Use expanded vocabulary and descriptive words in oral and written responses to simple texts.

I15. Read simple poetry and use simple sentences in answering factual comprehension questions.

Early Advanced

Word Analysis

EA1. Use common English morphemes to derive meaning in oral and silent reading (e.g., basic syllabication rules, regular and irregular plurals, and basic phonics).

EA2. Recognize sound/symbol relationship and basic word-formation rules in phrases, simple sentences, or simple text.

Fluency and Systematic Vocabulary Development

EA3. Recognize simple antonyms and synonyms (e.g., *good, bad; blend, mix*) in stories or games.

EA4. Use simple prefixes and suffixes when they are attached to known vocabulary.
EA5. Use decoding skills and knowledge of academic and social vocabulary to begin independent reading.

Reading Comprehension
EA6. Read text and use detailed sentences to identify orally the main idea and use the idea to draw inferences about the text.
EA7. Read stories and orally respond to them by answering factual comprehension questions about cause-and-effect relationships.
EA8. Write a brief summary (three or four complete sentences) of a story.
EA9. Read and use basic text features, such as the title, table of contents, and chapter headings.
EA10. Read stories and texts from content areas and respond orally to them by restating facts and details to clarify ideas.

Literary Response and Analysis
EA11. Read short poems and orally identify the basic elements (e.g., rhythm and rhyme).
EA12. Read a literary selection and orally identify the literary elements of plot, setting, and character.
EA13. Read a story and identify the beginning, middle, and end.

Writing Standards

Beginning
Writing Strategies
B1. Copy the English alphabet legibly.
B2. Copy word posted and commonly used in the classroom (e.g., labels, number names, days of the week).
B3. Write a few words or phrases about an event or character from a story read by the teacher.
B4. Write a phrase or simple sentence about an experience generated from a group story.

Early Intermediate
Writing Strategies
EI1. Write simple sentences about events or characters from familiar stories read aloud by the teacher.
EI2. Write simple sentences by using key words posted and commonly used in the classroom [e.g., labels, number names, days of the week, and months (e.g., "Today is Tuesday")].
EI3. Write one to two simple sentences (e.g., "I went to the park").

Intermediate
Writing Strategies
I1. Write short narrative stories that include the elements of setting and characters.
I2. Produce independent writing that is understood when read but may include inconsistent use of standard grammatical forms.
I3. Following a model, proceed through the writing process to independently write short paragraphs of at least three lines.
I4. Write simple sentences appropriate for language arts and other content areas (e.g., math, science, social studies).
I5. Write a friendly letter of a few lines.

Early Advanced
Writing Strategies
EA1. Write short narratives that include elements of setting, characters, and events.
EA2. Proceed through the writing process to write short paragraphs that maintain a consistent focus.
EA3. Use complex vocabulary and sentences appropriate for language arts and other content areas (e.g., math, science, social studies).
EA4. Write a formal letter.
EA5. Produce independent writing with consistent use of standard grammatical forms. (Some rules may not be followed.)

Listening and Speaking Standards

Beginning
Strategies and Applications
B1. Begin to speak a few words or sentences by using some English phonemes and rudimentary English grammatical forms (e.g., single words or phrases).
B2. Answer simple questions with one- to two-word responses.
B3. Respond to simple directions and questions by using physical actions and other means of nonverbal communication (e.g., matching objects, pointing to an answer, drawing pictures).
B4. Independently use common social greetings and simple repetitive phrases (e.g., "Thank you", "You're welcome").

Early Intermediate
Strategies and Applications
EI1. Begin to be understood when speaking but may have some inconsistent use of standard English grammatical forms and sounds (e.g., plurals, simple past tense, pronouns such as *he* or *she*).

EI2. Ask and answer questions by using phrases or simple sentences.

EI3. Retell familiar stories and short conversations by using appropriate gestures, expressions, and illustrative objects.

EI4. Orally communicate basic needs (e.g., "May I get a drink?").

EI5. Recite familiar rhymes, songs, and simple stories.

Intermediate

Strategies and Applications

I1. Ask and answer instructional questions by using simple sentences.

I2. Listen attentively to stories and information and identify important details and concepts by using both verbal and nonverbal responses.

I3. Make oneself understood when speaking by using consistent standard English grammatical forms and sounds; however, some rules may not be followed (e.g., third-person singular, male and female pronouns).

I4. Participate in social conversations with peers and adults on familiar topics by asking and answering questions and soliciting information.

I5. Retell stories and talk about school-related activities by using expanded vocabulary, descriptive words, and paraphrasing.

Early Advanced

Strategies and Applications

EA1. Listen attentively to stories and information and orally identify key details and concepts.

EA2. Retell stories in greater detail by including the characters, setting, and plot.

EA3. Make oneself understood when speaking by using consistent standard English grammatical forms, sounds, intonation, pitch, and modulation but may make random errors.

EA4. Participate in and initiate more extended social conversations with peers and adults on unfamiliar topics by asking and answering questions and restating and soliciting information.

EA5. Recognize appropriate ways of speaking that vary according to the purpose, audience, and subject matter.

EA6. Ask and answer instructional questions with more extensive supporting elements (e.g., "Which part of the story was the most important?").

English-Language Conventions

Beginning

English Language Conventions

B5. Use capitalization when writing one's own name.

Early Intermediate

English Language Conventions

EI4. Use capitalization to begin sentences and for proper nouns.

EI5. Use a period or question mark at the end of a sentence.

EI6. Edit writing for basic conventions (e.g., capitalization and use of periods) and make some corrections.

Intermediate

English Language Conventions

I6. Produce independent writing that may include some inconsistent use of capitalization, periods, and correct spelling.

I7. Use standard word order but may have some inconsistent grammatical forms (e.g., subject/verb without inflections).

Early Advanced

English Language Conventions

EA6. Produce independent writing that may include some periods, correct spelling, and inconsistent capitalization.

EA7. Use standard word order with some inconsistent grammar forms (e.g., subject/verb agreement).

EA8. Edit writing to check some of the mechanics of writing (e.g., capitalization and periods).

Credits

Illustrations

8, 114, 160, 228 Marilyn Janovitz; 14, 108, 204 Donna Bizjak; 20, 32 Liisa Guida; 26, 76, 96 Wednesday Kirwan; 38, 64 Ann Iosa; 46, 70, 102, 146, 184 Anette Heiberg; 52, 128 Diane Greenseid; 58 David Preiss; 84 Jane Smith; 90, 152 Sharon Vargo; 122, 134 Sarah Beise; 140 Janet McDonnell; 166, 190 Dani Jones; 172, 216 Deb Johnson; 178 Scott Rolf; 198 Robbie Short; 210, 222 Liz Goulet Dubois

Photographs

Every effort has been made to secure permission and provide appropriate credit for photographic material. The publisher deeply regrets any omission and pledges to correct errors called to its attention in subsequent editions.

Unless otherwise acknowledged, all photographs are the property of Pearson Education, Inc.

Photo locators denoted as follows: Top (T), Center (C), Bottom (B), Left (L), Right (R), Background (Bkgd).

2 ©Douglas Menuez/Riser/Getty Images; 8 (CL) ©Matt Henry Gunther/Getty Images, (TL) ©David Young-Wolff/Stone/Getty Images, (CL) ©Purestock/Alamy, (BL) ©Ambient Images Inc./Alamy Images; 10 (TR) Howard Shooter/©DK Images, (TL, BL, BC, BR) Getty Images, (TC) ©Jana Leon/Getty Images; 11 (T) Getty Images, (B) ©Design Pics Inc./Alamy; 13 ©Jupiter Images/Creatas/Alamy; 14 (TL) ©Jupiter Images/Creatas/Alamy, (TL) Geoff Dann/©DK Images, (TL) Dave King/©DK Images, (TL) Peter Chadwick/©DK Images; 16 (CL) Getty Images, (CR) ©Westend61/Getty Images, (CR) ©Corbis/Jupiter Images, (BL) Dave King/©DK Images; 17 (B) ©JLP/Jose L. Pelaez/Corbis, (T) ©Alexander Nicholson/Photonica/Getty Images; 19 ©Corbis Super RF/Alamy; 20 Getty Images; 22 (CL) ©D. Hurst/Alamy Images, (CR) ©Jupiter Images/Polka Dot/Alamy, (TL) ©Matt Gray/Taxi/Getty Images, (TR) ©Matt Carr/Photonica/Getty Images; 23 (T) ©MIXA Co., Ltd./Alamy, (B) ©Lauren Burke/Getty Images; 25 ©Blend Images/Getty Images; 26 (TL) ©VCL/Spencer Rowell/Getty Images, (TL) ©Martin Riedl/Getty Images, (TL) ©Alex Mares-Manton/Asia Images/Getty Images, (TL) Getty Images; 29 (B) ©blue jean images/Getty Images, (T) Getty Images; 31 ©age fotostock/SuperStock; 32 (TL) ©Suk-Heui Park/Photographer's Choice/Getty Images, (TL) Getty Images, (TL) ©Corbis/Jupiter Images; 34 (TL, TCL, TCR) Dave King/©DK Images, (TC) Philip Dowell/©DK Images, (TR, TC) ©DK Images; 35 (B) ©Steve Satushek/Getty Images, (T) ©Pacific Stock/SuperStock; 37 ©Kevin Dodge/Corbis; 38 (TL) ©Johnny Greig/Alamy Images, (TL) ©Dorothy Young Riess M.D./Workbook Stock/Jupiter Images, (TL) ©Jupiter Images/Comstock Images/Alamy, (TL) ©George Hall/Corbis, (TL) Lynton Gardiner/©DK Images; 40 (TL) ©Tetra Images/Alamy, (TCL) Mike Dunning/©DK Images, (TCR) Richard Leeney/©DK Images, (CL) ©Construction Photography/Corbis; 41 (T) Jupiter Images, (B) ©Jim West/Alamy Images; 43 ©Ian Shaw/Alamy Images; 46 (TL) ©William Manning/Corbis, (TL) ©Tim Street-Porter/Beateworks/Corbis; 48 (CC) Getty Images, (TR) Roger Smith/©DK Images, (TC) Craig Knowles/©DK Images, (TCL) Clive Boursnell/©DK Images, (TR) ©DEA/F. Luccese/De Agostini Picture Library/Getty Images, (CR) ©Frans Lemmens/Iconica/Getty Images; 49 (B) ©Corbis Premium RF/Alamy, (T) Steve Gorton/©DK Images; 51 ©Martin Brigdale/Dorling Kindersley/Getty Images; 52 (TL) ©Cydney Conger/Corbis, (TL) ©Hans Reinhard/zefa/Corbis, (TL) ©Ariel Skelley/Corbis, (TL) Tim Ridley/©DK Images; 54 (TC, TCR) Getty Images, (TL, CC) ©DK Images, (TCL) Tim Ridley/©DK Images; 55 (TC) ©Claus Meyer/Minden Pictures/Getty Images, (BC) ©Gerry Bishop/Visuals Unlimited; 57 ©Claudia Adams/Alamy Images; 58 (TL) ©J & B Photographers/Animals Animals/Earth Scenes, (TL) ©Roger De La Harpe/Animals Animals/Earth Scenes, (TL) Getty Images, (TL) ©DK Images; 60 (TL) Jane Burton/©DK Images, (CC) Gordon Clayton/©DK Images, (TCL) ©DK Images, (CC) Bill Ling/©DK Images, (CR) ©Pat Doyle/Corbis; 61 (TC) ©Konrad Wothe/Science Faction/Getty Images, (BC) ©Jorg & Petra Wegner/Animals Animals/Earth Scenes; 63 ©Art Wolfe/Getty Images; 64 ©Henry King/Photonica/Getty Images; 66 (TL) ©Phyllis Greenberg/Animals Animals/Earth Scenes, (TC) Ken Preston-Mafham/Animals Animals/Earth Scenes, (CC) ©Richard Day/Animals Animals/Earth Scenes, (CR) ©Kevin Schafer/Corbis, (CL) ©Arthur Gurmankin /Visuals Unlimited, (TR) ©Edwin Giesbers/Foto Natura/Getty Images; 67 (TC) ©Stouffer Productions/Animals Animals/Earth Scenes, (BC) ©Suzi Eszterhas/Animals Animals/Earth Scenes; 69 ©Tom J. Ulrich/Visuals Unlimited; 70 (TL) ©A & M Shah/Animals Animals/Earth Scenes, (TL) ©E. Bartov/OSF/Animals Animals/Earth Scenes, (TL) ©Craig Tuttle/Corbis, (TL) Ray Moller/©DK Images; 72 (TL) ©Image Source, (TR) ©Larry Dale Gordon/Photographer's Choice/Getty Images; 73 (BC) ©Frank Cezus/Taxi/Getty Images, (TC) ©O. Newman/OSF/Animals Animals/Earth Scenes; 75 ©Joe McDonald/Corbis; 76 (TL) ©DLILLC/Corbis, (TL) ©Mike Powell/Stone+/Getty Images; 78 (CC) ©Cultura/Alamy, (TCR) ©Design Pics Inc./Alamy, (TR) ©Jupiter Images/Comstock Images/Alamy, (TL) ©Patrick Molnar/The Image Bank/Getty Images, (TC) ©LWA-Dann Tardif/Corbis, (CL) ©David Stoecklein/Corbis; 79 (TC) ©Joe McDonald/Animals Animals/Earth Scenes, (BC) ©Ana Laura Gozalez/Animals Animals/Earth Scenes; 81 ©Renee Lynn/Corbis; 84 (TL) ©Norbert Schaefer/Corbis, (TL) ©Image100/Jupiter Images, (TL) ©Tomas Rodriguez/Solas Photography/Veer, Inc.; 86 ©Jupiter Images/Brand X/Alamy; 87 (B) Corbis, (T) ©Jupiter Images/Brand X/Alamy; 89 Getty Images; 90 (TL) ©Nik Wheeler/Corbis, (TL) ©altrendo nature/Getty Images; 92 (CR) ©Elyse Lewin/Getty Images, (TR) ©Jupiter Images/Brand X/Alamy, (CR) ©Jupiter Images/BananaStock/Alamy, (TL) ©Donna Day/Corbis; 93 (T) ©Purestock/Alamy, (B) ©Nancy Sheehan/PhotoEdit; 95 ©Blend Images/Alamy; 96 (TL) ©John Lund/Stone/Getty Images, (TL) ©Glow Images/Alamy, (TL) ©Blend Images/Getty Images, (TL) ©Blend Images/Jupiter Images; 98 (TR) ©Lance Burnell/Alamy Images, (TCL) ©David Stuckel/Alamy Images, (TCR) ©Lynn Seldon/Danita Delimont, Agent, (TL) ©Ron & Patty Thomas/Getty Images; 99 (B) The Granger Collection, NY, (T) ©Scherl/SV-Bilderdienst/The Image Works, Inc.; 101 The Granger Collection, NY; 102 (TL) ©Bob Daemmrich/The Image Works, Inc., (TL) Getty Images; 104 (TC) ©Rick & Nora Bowers/Alamy Images, (TCR) ©Breck P. Kent/Animals Animals/Earth Scenes, (TL) ©Guy Motil/Flirt Photography/Veer, Inc., (TCL) ©Altrendo Nature/Getty Images, (TR) ©Julian Deghy/Alamy Images; 105 (B) ©Steve Skjold /Alamy Images, (T) Getty Images; 107 ©Simon Marcus/Corbis; 108 (TL) ©Judith Collins/Alamy, (TL) ©Jupiter Images/Brand X/Alamy; 110 (TL) ©Supapixx/Alamy, (TCL) Jupiter Images, (CC) Stockdisc, (TCR) ©Gregor Schuster/Getty Images, (TR) Dave King/©DK Images; 111 (C) ©Rubberball/Punchstock, (B) ©David Pollack/Corbis, (T) The Granger

Handbook

Aa Bb Cc Dd Ee Ff Gg Hh Ii Jj Kk Ll Mm
Nn Oo Pp Qq Rr Ss Tt Uu Vv Ww Xx Yy Zz

0 1 2 3 4 5 6 7 8 9

The Alphabet cards can help you
with sounds in English.

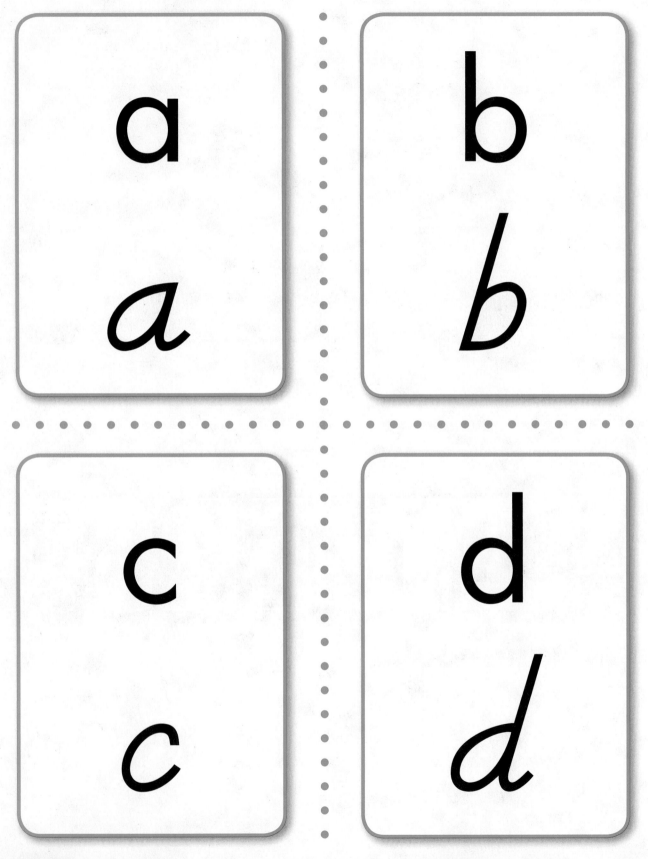

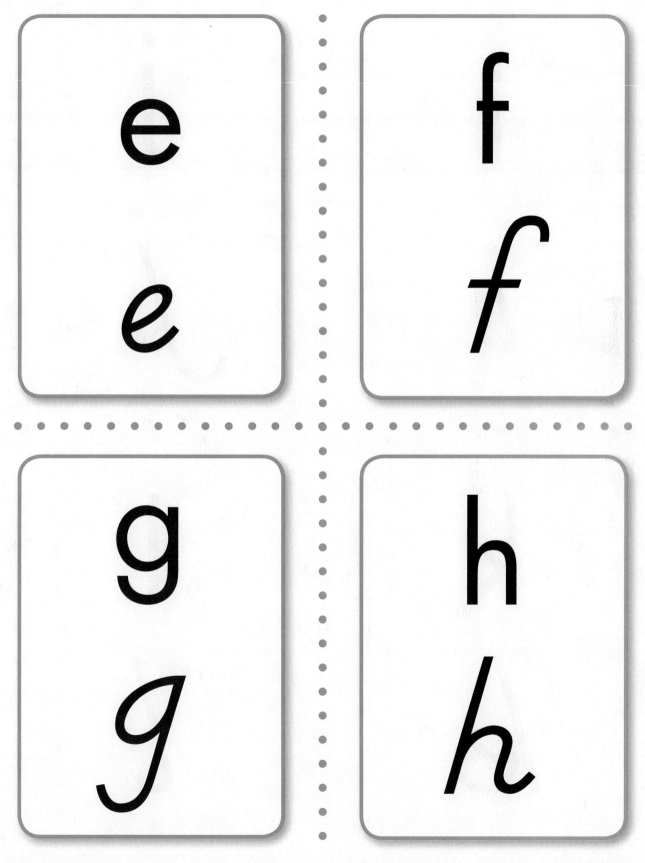

e e

f f

g g

h h

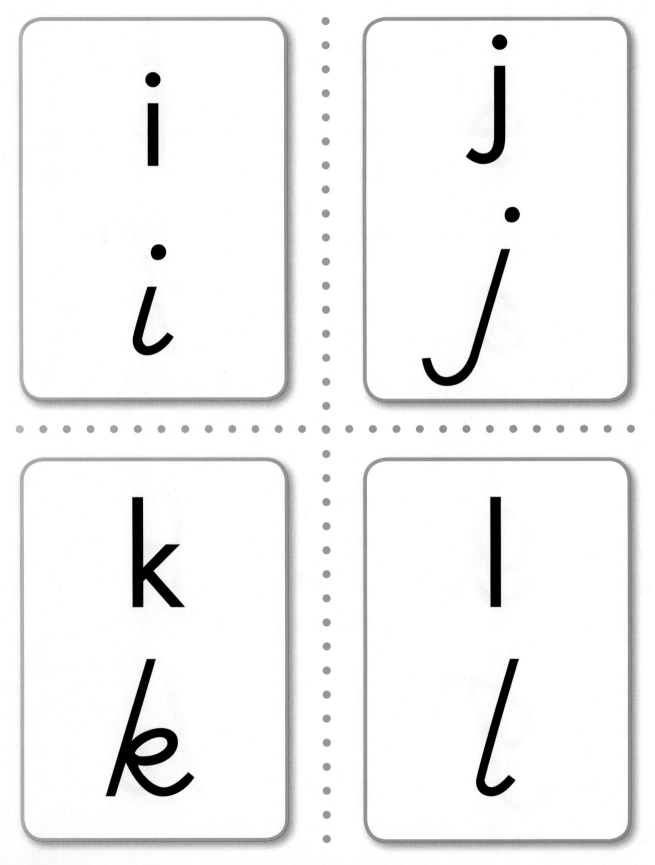

i
i

j
j

k
k

l
l

AC•4

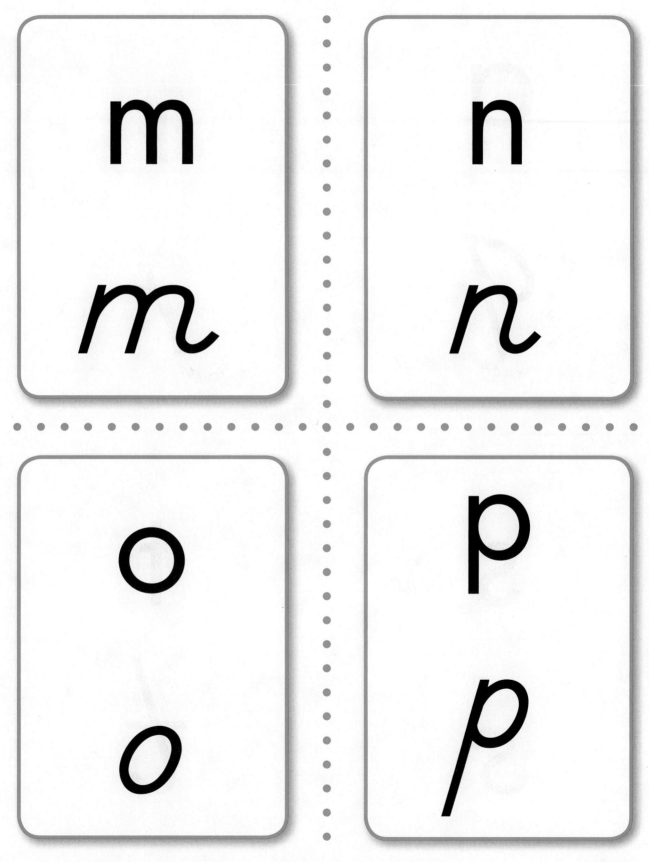

m

m

n

n

o

o

p

p

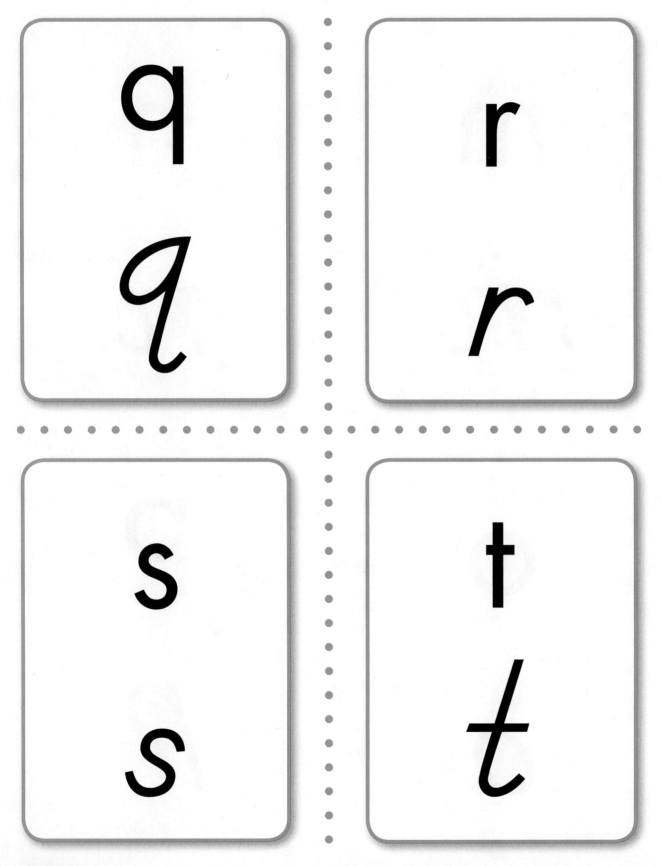

q q

r r

s s

t t

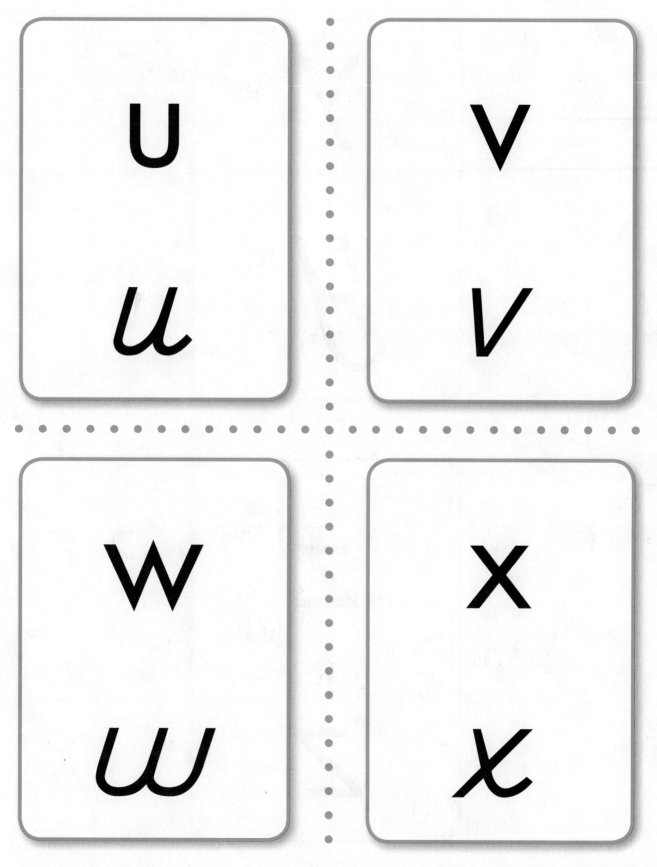

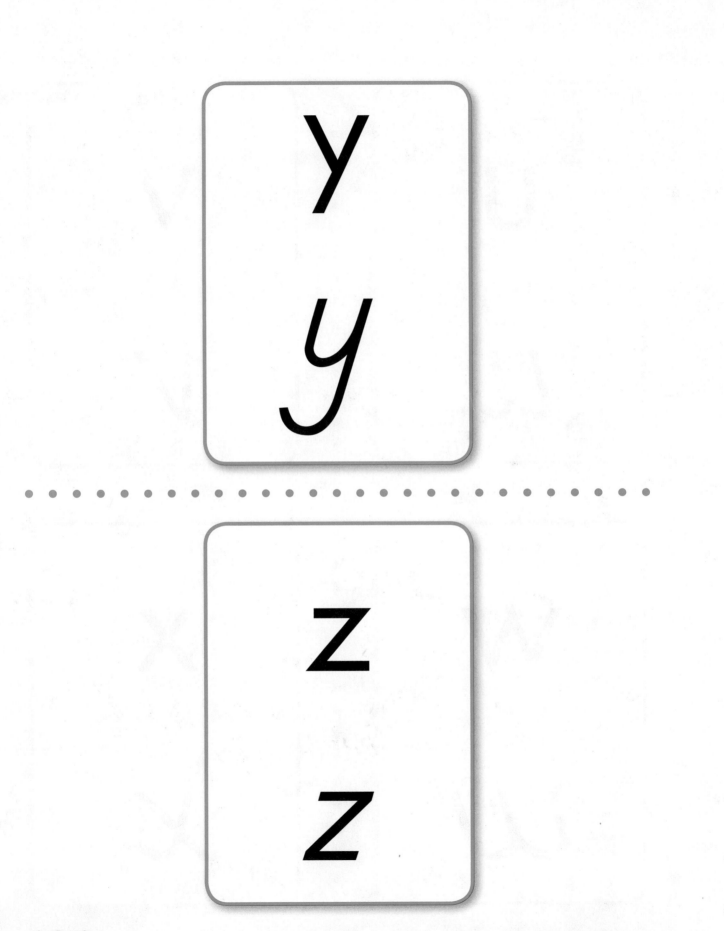